Suits for the Swarm

Suits *for the* Swarm

Matt Gano

Carlos & Annie,
Hope you like these
old poems about growing
up, and speaking up.
Much love,
Matt Gano

MoonPath Press

Poetry
ISBN 978-1-936657-10-0

Cover photo by Sue Gano
Author photos by Laura Totten

Design by Tonya Namura
using Liberation Serif

MoonPath Press is dedicated to publishing the
best poets of the U.S. Northwest Pacific states

MoonPath Press
PO Box 1808
Kingston, WA 98346

MoonPathPress@yahoo.com

http://MoonPathPress.com

For my mom,who taught me how to write.

For my dad, and all the head-stories.

Acknowledgments

Huge debt of gratitude to my mentors and the space they've offered under their wings: Jim Bertolino, Roberto Ascalon, Aaron Counts, Iyeoka Okoawo, Karen Finneyfrock, Daemond Arrindell, Christa Bell, Mike McGee.

Many thanks to my family and community, for all who've shown me love and inspired me to keep following the writing. Mom and Dad (Ken and Sue) and Jake and Laura Gano, Grandma Kay Gano, Sherry, Rob, Ryan, Alec, and Larry Mandell, Lauren Bishop, Chris Carroll, Jared Hayes, Cetan Wanbli Williams, Danny Sherrard, Buddy Wakefield, John Murillo, Kathleen Flenniken, Anis Mojgani, Jack McCarthy, Jeanann Verlee, Jon Sands, Samantha Thornhill, Rajnii Eddins, Brian Capobianchi, Mahogany Brown, Denise Jolly, Tara Hardy, Laura Totten, Steven Clough, Greg Brisendine, Sara Brickman, John Burgess, Robert Huston, Jon Greenberg, Dean Ferguson, Kristin Bailey-Fogerty, Hollis Wong-Wear, Madeline Clifford, Chris Zweigle, Angela Dy, Leighton Overson, Kevin Smith, Weston Jandacka, Jake Clifford, Jake Edens and many more I'm forgetting…

Great amount of thanks to the organizations and schools that have given me opportunity to share my craft: Writers In The Schools, Youth Speaks, Arts Corps, The Julliard School, Lee Shau Kee School of Creativity, Richard Hugo House, Skagit River Poetry Project, Western Washington University, Esalen Institute.

Lastly, a very special and huge thanks to Lana Hechtman Ayers at MoonPath Press for taking a chance on a kid from the sticks.

Table of Contents

Suits *for the* Swarm

One

Serious Business

I asked you to share
your poetry and you told me,

"Okay,
but only
if you don't
make fun of me."

It prompts the question:
How much does *fun*
go for retail these days?

They say it's made
at someone else's expense
like commerce, so cheap
laughs are easy pickin'
in the bargain bin
and I'm a sucker for a discount,
but I won't make fun of you
Darlin', as long as we can make this fun
'cause *poetry* has become serious
business.

Serious like a bee suit,
or red ties on Sundays,
that kind of serious.

Fun comes in two buckets.
One is for the sand crabs
and the other is castle
construction, broken

plastic handles, heavy-wet
sand, the type that tides
melt over beach fires
to petrify calligraphy
on the coast of a new day.

And if you make fun of *me*
for sayin' these types of things
I might have to just laugh along.

I might be forced to blaze
down my forest of insecurities
and forage for truffles
under what's burnt.

I might lift a finger
to my inner dialogue,
might take all my casings off
strip clean, reset my being
'cause I've been washing fun
in my oven with giant bubble soap,
the kind that gets serious in your eye
when it pops your hope.

I've been so serious that fun
has become a four letter word.
I've had to add a "D"
because it always comes down to money.
     Like illness comes down
or shit comes down the pipe
     like walls come down

or goose pillows come
down.

The gravity is serious and weight
is serious, (ask Atkins in an afterlife)

and "wait" is serious,
ask about reparations,
seriously, ask yourself

what are you waiting for?

I've gone through
so many changes you could call me
alter-boy. I've never been
to a confession booth, but I live
for reasons to go there,
and if there's one place
on this earth I'd want my voice
to be heard, it's beyond
the confines, peaked
on a mountain range booming haiku
'til my tongue bleeds,
or the snow melts,
which ever comes first.

I'm yellin' knock-knock
jokes to my echo
just to hear, "who's there,"
and my answer;

I am two arms and a pair of legs
planted on this mountaintop,
an aspen in morning, a hand wave
to the sun and middle finger
to darkness. I'm double barrel-
chested with lungs that pack punch
like a third grade field trip.

I'm a heavy heart
scrapin' the scales
with a voice like a violin
in need of tuning

I'm here.

I'm two steps away
from dancing like I mean it.
I'm smoke and lights.
I'm two handfuls of chalk
open to a gust,
I'm the leopard print
on the plain's shadow

I'm here, a tangible speck in this vastness.

My knees are knockin' up
a cloud of frost with a jaw
propped by a blue tongue,
bitten with cold,
and affirmations keep me tastin'

but I still don't know
when to let go of that echo.

So Darlin',
I won't make fun of you,
'cause a voice only carries
as far as someone cradles it
and it's okay to admit
that we all
got growin'
to do.

Torpedoes

My love for my brother
came with cuts.
Thin gashes on our shins
chasing grasshoppers
through tumbleweed.

We'd herd them
through cheat-grass,
ceremoniously
remove them
from the collection
jar, one at a time
and spike them
on our porch.

It kept them
stunned.

We tore legs
from torsos,
made them
torpedoes, meals
for our goldfish,
and for praying
mantis we picked
from the lavender.

In the dead of July,
summer lays the day

down late, and we stay
up, until the Dipper
appears.

The Wrecking Point

It was always Sunday.
We had bikes and plenty
of gears but wanted wheelies
and tricks, danger and more speed.

Thomson's Hill is a pregnant belly,
a high mound for the young to take.
It is soft desert silt and ancient
softball stones left from glaciers
that carved the Columbia.

We rode there, through orchards
into Panoramic Heights, high
from the road. We wore adventure
instead of helmets.

We parked on a ledge
and lorded over our small town.
Sized up an access rode
running vertical down the face.

Kevin dared me to bomb
down with no brakes (actually
told me not to which was
pretty much the same)
so I weighted the pedals
and let go, full-mountain charge.

I was on my way to legend
with speed shoving from behind

when the trail-dust lifted
its powder veil. Old boulders
ate my rims, flung me
donkey over handlebars
into a hot cloud
at the bottom.

Kevin rolled slow
to the wrecking point,
checked me for blood
as I moaned like a zombie
in search of brains

and felt the hill
in my stomach.

Extractor

Purple dusk
clouds and dust.
Honeybees fan wings
for warmth, flexing pulses
of pollen. Thorax electric hive.

Crack the seal,
beeswax with putty
knife, Dad pops propolis
pulling honey-fat frames.

The garage fills
with harvest, death-air
sweetness, hot blade bees
drowning in their own honey.

Load the wagon,
a Radio Flyer playing
white noise down the road.

Jake and I hock
honey to the neighbors
Dad lets us keep the money
and we get along like brothers

until we get home.

How to Rule

Start by building an RC-car racetrack
on the empty lot next to your house.

Don't let any of the neighbors
play with it. Only you
and Big Kevin can touch it.

Tell your little brother
he's not old enough,
and to go back inside,
then mock him when he cries.

Tell Eric, the kid
from across the cul-de-sac
to fuck off and go home
'cause if he helps you build it,
you can tell, he'll be playin'
on your track all the time
without permission.

Never take *shit* from anyone
younger than you, regardless of size.
Big kids rule and bigger in age
is all that matters.

On the bus home from school
learn how to say and properly project
phrases like, eat-shit shit-eater,
suck my dick, and butt fucker,
from Craig, the Mormon kid.

Apply these insults timely
to anyone who dares
to step on your racetrack.

This will spark a block feud
with Eric and his ally, Justin
(another punk kid from next door).
Battle with dirt clods. When Eric says
he'll box you to settle it.
Accept in an instant.

Land a hundred left jabs
and walk him in circles
around his garage that reeks
like wet hockey equipment.

Punch his nose 'til he quits.
Slam the gloves on the concrete.
Laugh in his face then leave
when his older brother threatens
to kick your ass and calls Eric a pussy.

Always stand up for your own
little brother, even if he annoys
the shit out of you.

When he comes home crying
because Eric and Justin threw
him in the arborvitae, run outside
and punch Eric in the eye.

Feel the knuckle
of your thumb sink
into his fat socket.

Let his eye-squish remind you
of testing biscuit dough.
Tell them both,
with spit on your lips,

"nobody makes my brother cry…
                              but me!"

Launching the Whale

My dad is a carpenter,
sort of like Jesus,
but he doesn't believe in God.

His holy space is drills and grinders,
roaring teeth spitting chips and dust.

When I was twelve we built a canoe
from strips of cedar,
ripped boards for weeks.

The frame in the garage
was scaled like an empty whale,
bones lurching from the shop floor.
We arced on its new skin
with glue and heavy staples.

Dad wore a green down-vest
like a turtle shell, he said
it would comfort our shop-mammal
to be built by something familiar.

As the frame was full with hull and keel,
we plied out staples like final stitches
removed from a recovered experiment,
ran our hands down its sanded spine,
the work painting into our palms,
our pores absorbing the bonding.

When we rode the whale,
we launched it from the shore
like pushing a dead cow back into the sea,
boots in the shallows filled with lake water.

It would take us to the middle
where the big fish are,
where the casting rods
bend like cottonwood over glass,
dance jigs, whippin' back and forth.
Dragon tongues.

This is how we sit –
me, navigator bow-boy,
front paddle like the steam engine
is tug boat, but little boat.
Dad is stern, rudder man,
power in the deep dig,
he spanked the water good,
like it forgot to take the garbage out.

We pull the trash from the beaver dens
and replace them with good sticks,
he says they don't know any better, the babies
will get the soda rings around their heads
like the Spanish inquisition and die slow.

We don't want 'em to die slow.
    "Keep rowing,

hard on the left,
      watch out for the log!"

I see the log.
The log looks like a floating dog.
Put my paddle in it, it sank through
like a fork in cat food.
It is/*was* a dog,
belly stickin' out
like helium and rot.

See how the K9's are chipped and peeled back?
Musta' been eatin' marmots.
Sometimes a stray dog will eat rocks
if it's hungry enough.

My dad is a scientist.
He doesn't believe in god.
His holy space is lakes and bug guts,
they cell through him when we walk on the roots
and slipping path of the Yakima valley.

We Swiss-blade open on the pond,
make ripples like loons,
hoot-hoot against the quarry for the echo.
Make campfire dance
with pucker-mouth lip wind
and sizzle up the iron-pan
washin' in mountain water.

When the tent gots the squirts with dew
and embers burn down, crackin'
like mosquitoes on Dad's neck
with his slappin', and it's dark as bears,
morning peeps over the ridge
and we are simple
heirloom pocketknives,
carving memory into the tree.

Silvers

The son of a bitch
went limp
when I let him
off the hook.

Put my heel
on his throat
raw gill pulsing
a veteran wound
like he wanted
his bayonet
anatomy,
to be gutted,
slow roasted
in parchment,
with garlic,
put to work.

The funeral-blue
corrugated boat floor
knows blood,
exactly how
the dead float.

Quince

Grandpa wore sawdust,
mahogany and flannel,
wore callused palms
shaping wood into time
pieces for peace at home.

He bent with the quince tree,
pruning through seasons.
Never missed a chance to tell me
how rare it is to see one.

Dairyman, he carried milk,
collected thirty years
on those door steps
kicked a couple dogs,
enjoyed the job.

In the garage
he taught tools and —man,
sharpened chisels and blades.
History flew, stories
like hot sparks
over his shoulder.

We spoke last
as he reclined in
his favorite rocking chair,
he said he was happy
that he was still
here.

Ninety-three years, no senile
but went blind 'bout ten back
couldn't see
couldn't fix
or make things
no more.

Grandma is ninety-four
he's her new azalea.

She went to wake him
shook soft, he was gone
Grandma, pragmatic,
matter of fact
told us,
Dad just died.

A day from Valentine's
and the roses are unusual
for February.

Three uncles
my dad
four sons

a casket.
Careful,
place him
on the grave
frame.

The plot, a part
in his favorite joke
he'd say,
"look how popular
the place is—

people are dying

to get in here"

Ready-Made

Our God is an awesome God
he reigns from heaven above

Around the fire pit, at the end of a jetty
pointed like a sassy tongue
into the ocean, I was corralled
for my voice, confirmed
without permission
to lend my lungs and belt loud
into slick-dark.

At the turn of the third verse
as the song reached steeple,
the sky burst into torrent
thundering something awesome.

> I was 14, on an isolated island
> off the coast of Vancouver BC
> at Jesus camp.
>
> This was my first experience
> with organized religion
> and it was straight-up hard-core
> super-Christ.
>
> My mom sent me there on accident,
> unaware of the circumstances.
> My Jewish mother, guilty
> to this day wears her grief
> like a quilt of wet papyrus.

Oh, the heavens rained!
Our congregation fled
for the mess hall slipping
and flailing frantically.
In unison, our group
was jolted to the mud
with a lighting bolt
whip-cracked behind us.

This abrupt halt to reverence,
the shut-up of my forced worship
was all I needed to convince me
that our counselors, bent
on bringing the "born-again,"
had yet to be "forgiven"
and should not
have been leading
an invocation of such
for adolescents with
unanswered questions.

We are told to search high,
but we are all ready-made
celestial. Iridescent.

Elemental. Death
does not bring us
closer. We are living
parts

of the sky.

Trespass

For Justin

We cloaked in dark navy,
our bags obese with Rust-O's,
fat-caps and thins,
we were as big as we could be.

The faint clacking of cans
called to rattlesnakes coiled
in the rockery like land mines.

In the desert night, the sagebrush
rose from its haunches to follow our trail,
sweep out our footprints, take our names,
hold them under its tongue, between its teeth
like a Darkling beetle in its jaw.

We hung to the dirt and gravel path
down iron tracks into the train tunnel
to throw our mistakes and masterpieces
up on cooling concrete walls
on tip-toe, to extend our radius.

The hissing aerosol mocked reptile.
We painted with trespass, impermanence,
knowing with countless coats of cover up
our names would be buffed
deep into the city.

Two

Cataracts

A man goes blind today.
His name is Darrell.
He struggles through the door
of this bank like I struggle
getting out of it.

He ambles up to my window,
he's having trouble
finding his balance.

I'm a teller, it's my job
to explain to customers
how they get in the red
or how much they are in the black,
and pretend to shed light
on the grey areas.

Darrell is a regular customer
but he doesn't come in often.
He's hoping I'm open.

I've watched his vision
decline, a semi with no brakes.
He looks me in the eye,
blinks at my foggy silhouette
he's been slipping into shadow,
his voice shimmies, a 50's pickup
revved with frustration.

He says,
"I wasn't born this way"
tells me he is preparing
for the dark, learning
to swing a cane before his eyes
break down. Been practicing
his brail, learning to read by feeling.

He slides three cards in the tray,
tells me to pick one for ID.
I can't accept any of them.

While he roots through his things,
I wait, staring blindly
into my own reflection
on the inside of the glass
and think to myself.
I look tired
and need a haircut.

Somewhere in between
regularity and repetition
compassion curdles
like milk in whiskey,
but somehow it seeps in, slower
now like I'm Novocain
enriched, just a dull pressure.

Been building a natural casing,
a callus, or cataracts
like Darrell.

Seizure on Eastlake

Yesterday my car had a stroke.
The check engine light has been
crying wolf for months.

It seized in the middle of traffic,
fell to the floor, electrodes
jerking like legs out of sequence, eyelids
flickering at the green arrow on Eastlake.

The road was full of takers,
tired of the rain, full of bus,
full of workday and longing for home,
for their stir-fry or baked chicken
on a Friday.

The looks in their eyes
as they passed said, "walk your cripple,
your debilitated jalopy out of here,
we are rush-hour-mad,
with middle fingers and fangs."

In return, we waved with inconvenience,
no flares or hazards. The blood-filling-serpent
of vehicles stacking back to the bridge.

A meter-maid whipped his buggy alongside
and charged up to the window,
cop knock knuckles rapping like an accusation.
His ticket-giver instincts turned him frantic
demanding we move immediately.

With bureaucratic tongue he flapped
that he was not actually a police officer,
and could do nothing to help.

Above, the overpass hummed hard
like a cliff full of swallows.
We sat waiting for the flatbed, the big gurney,
counting minutes like checking a pulse
I shook the steering wheel and said,
"don't be scared,
I hate you,

god damn it."

Noon

The church bells
make the Steller's jays
crazy

make 'em caw storm
in the lawn

blue back
blue sky
rally bike beak

bells sound chorus
hours counted
birds keep time   on their own
it is spatial
how they
do it

when they go in a fit
bantering out the stillness
count the shrill yelps
          hard harmony

the jays are recalcitrant.

The city reverbs
their revolt.

Music Maker

Maybe it starts
in the bed of a pickup
or maybe it's out in space
some dust particle ion-charged
pulling it all together.

Maybe it's in our gums
and the way they bleed
when floss is applied
or the way a baby tooth
aches like childbirth
before it's yanked free,
when blood vessels
are released to run veins
like a dog track.

Optimist
is so close to
optometrist,
  always looking
  for the best way
  to see things.

  Stay focused.
This is about miracles.

 The anointing water
 is hatching mosquitoes
 mosquitoes are biting
 the holy trinity
 the holy trinity is bumpy now

and itchy from bites,
bites are growing
as the holy trinity
can't resist scratching them,
the scratch marks
resemble the lashings
on Jesus.

(There's a miracle in there
somewhere.)

Maybe it's between the slats
in the bed of that pickup
or where all that fancy stardust
is just grey lumps of spider imitator.

Maybe it's in the root
down to the nerve,
like how a chipped tooth
will tell you you have a face,
a holy-water face, three dimensional
this is your trinity,
your lashes holding in miracles
an optical Jesus
looking for the best way
to see things,
optimal
the body
sings audible
inside its case.

Miracle music maker,
put your ear to world.
Hear the tide break in your shell,
how incredibly wave you are.
Listen for the gulls in your gullet,
the chain clanging on the flagpole
waving your independence,
you driftwood-journey.

Listen to yourself go
fire siren loud
don't be alarmed,
it's the sound of awakening.
beep
    animal sound
             nothing sound
      om
   ding!
feel the cabin pressure
      hiss
        pop
      going up!

Can you hear the elevator music?
It's the radio in your frontal lobe,
the slight twang in your right brain
listen, catch the prism,
you are a rainbow xylophone

2nd grade symphony
the ping
        ping
            dong
beautiful melody that goes
      swing set
tire swing
      monkey bars on the music scales!

Shed your scales now bird, pretty rainbow
                  pretty prism
           spectrum
      spectacle
      see it clear optometrist!

Stay focused.

This about miracles,
what lenses we view
the world with
and silhouettes
in the bed of a pick-up truck
settling with the dust.

New Heat

The sun is running its fingers
through my houseplants.
Outside, East Madison runs
with motorcycle and morning.
Capitol Hill is roasted espresso
and always under construction.

When the clouds burn off
and the pavement dries,
it seems the sidewalks
are as tired of being slick
as the rest of us.

New heat pulls the black
from our clothes, a rare blue sky
pins our boots to the shoe rack.

We turn to shorts, we turn shirtless
at sixty four degrees, we turn
to the Sound, to the smell
of evergreen musk mixed
with salt from Elliott Bay.

The waves on Lake Washington
are happy to lap their dog-day tongues
onto attended beaches. The city
jitters in summer when it is too hot
for coffee, exactly how we like it.

To the Moon

(After Wallace Stevens, "Thirteen Ways of Looking at a Blackbird")

Hey moon,
yeah, I see you
glowing boomerang
glory-hole in the sky
rippling on the pond
and white.

Don't you know
you're the bastard asteroid
caught in our orbit?
Do you know
what the sun
calls your backside?

You are a neon-lily
in the funeral bouquet
of space.

Yeah, I see you,
with your lemon-meringue peaks
and eating-contest complexion.

Do you know
what the plankton
call your reflection?
Does it matter to you?
What's the matter?

How could you let us walk all over you?
    —naked in the street.
Even children stomp you
from still puddles,
they know your chalk-dust
tastes like powdered sugar
and tea cakes, you snicker doodle satellite
you cookie-pus sky-mantle,
dangling canvas begging
for our advertisements.

Silly billboard moon, USA moon,
flag-waver moon, patriot moon,
what a dutiful moon you are.

Go ahead: sleep late, moon.
Rest is good for the sacks
of pus mistaken for your eyes.
When you rise, shine
your Buddha belly on the tinted
windows of all our limos.
We will be toasting you.
Not because we love you,
nor because any of us notice
you are really here,
but because your libido tides
wash through our sex organs
like pipe music and the color
of our celebratory smoke
matches your skin tone.

Do you hear our howls
when you are full?
Gorged on the cycles,
we are ready to devour you
in ravenous moon-blood,
drill to your milk core
and douse ourselves in you
for new fetish porn.

Oh moon,
silly ship-guiding Galileo face,
crusty clown makeup on that stage.

Don't you know
your white wax will melt
under the spotlights?
That your pedestal will come
crashing down with the sky
when all our oxygen is gone?

The icecaps have turned their backs on you.
They are melting too, carving new oceans
in their rebellion. They will always
bear your resemblance.
Can you bare to see them go?

When we train wreck
into your craters and ditches
nurture us, crash-moon.

We will beg you for your bleach-face bed sheets
and hope for the renaissance
portrait of your breast to suckle
the night once again.

We, the Wild Horse

The earth wants to keep her diamonds
she knows our minds are full of soot,
she knows what we are looking for,
and that we're searching the wrong places.

Everything is pressed together tight,
all the lights are on and blinding,
we are deep in the mine but nothing is ours.

The streets are buckling because the earth is stuffed full,
the diamonds in her eyes are not for plucking.

There are legions of assholes who want
to pluck out the earth's eyes.

I am still a boy,
you are who you once were,
we are here together
wherever that will be,
I am not an imposter.
I have work to do, so do you.

The earth still wants us.

I want to finish more of what I've started,
be more garden-esque,
like the rake in the tool shed,
less like the shed
more like the tools,
I should actually stop being a tool.

Who am I fooling? Myself is easy
to pull the wool over,
my blankets are down and cozy,
I'm in there, some days, up to my nose past noon.
When rain does the streets like a cold disco
cars hustle down Madison, construction harps
on the morning hours, I sleep through it now,
not very sound
but I do it.

　　　Everything here is wild pony,
　　　outstretched empty-arm sky,
　　　thoroughbred plains seeking the edge.
　　　Everything here is running free,
　　　Nothing is in its place, disjointed braids,
　　　it's all amazing, nothing is insane.
　　　Everything here is wild pony,
　　　hourglass sky filling with bone dust
　　　a thorough breed, all the bases are covered
　　　the acids are in their places.
　　　My spine works against the grain
　　　it filters through the still,
　　　a silo fills with dust and bones,
　　　horsepower throws the lever to my eyelids.

I wake with diamonds in my eyes
and forget to write down my dreams.
I forget all the things I've considered,
but I know everything
that is new

is really old,
ancient even,
retold with shiny skin,
that the path to where I'm going
leads to places I've already been,
how amazing the scenery is.

Everything looks better with love on it.
The eyes of my lover are dark and soft
they remind me how vast and gentle the dark can be,
that there is someone waiting for my arrival,
who pulls me out of the mine,
who readies me for the still.

The clock in the photo-booth
never shows up in the stills,
still it is there, its hands
are winding us down
one flick at a time,
in the frame, the shadows
define us grainy, we consume
the grain, the earth
wants to keep her diamonds,
our minds, the love. The horses
in our sleep gallop out from the mine.

We are hard
and covered in soot,
but she wants us
anyway.

Ritual for Lovers

For Jake and Laura

We are here to witness the truth
you already know.
The ritual for lovers, is for us all
    to say we were present,
when you took each other's hands.
For you to say,
    "we were married then,
with celebration and tradition
    at our sides."

And here with the lasting proof
of love, found as close
as our mothers and fathers,
aunts and uncles, grandparents
and dear friends, you are next
to link with the longevity
and strength that makes us family.

And as your story continues
to shape new history, the script
of your memories is written
with the adventures you have told,
let all the land traveled together
become the distance
each of you are willing to go.

Let your love come easy,
in the unspoken,
in regular life moments.

Be reminded of the color
of her eyes in this light.
Let his love be every cliché
in the book and read aloud often.
Let the summer in August
always bring you back to now.
Let love find you simple,
  held gently around the waist
  dancing a slow circle
  in the kitchen
  to a memorized song.

Truth be Told

I want to know The Truth.
I mean I want to *know* it,
automatic as our breath
and definite as digestion,
know it like a limb, or an extra
appendage, a new erotic body part.

I want to know The Truth
like I know my mom
so it will be a   *nagging* truth.

I want to know The Truth
like it was a famous person,
know it like it was scandalous,
tabloid fat. then thin.
and fat again.

I want to know that it tried
Scientology and couldn't
go through with it.

There needs to be more publicity
for The Truth, fundraisers
and carwashes. We'll sell cookies
door-to-door and get signatures
from sponsors, who will pay us
to run a marathon for The Truth.

We can send The Truth
to Washington DC

for its senior class field trip
it's never   been there   before.

The Truth is being created now.
You can find it taped to the walls
of elementary school hallways,
drawn in crayon indigo
teaching that truth
is less of what we learn
and more in how we learn
to express it.

When we do it best,
it's made easy
like a milkshake
broken down and digestible,
but The Truth
can also be complex
and complicated

like electric stuff.

We should plug The Truth
into every socket and outlet
until we have an answer
to what is current. Let truth
be the pulse of our desire,
the fusion of ancient memory recall
with the future of imagination
to paint the world beautiful
in billions of different translations.

The Truth is only
what we make it out to be.

So let's make out with it!

Hardcore tongue kissing
like snakes humping.

We'll do it sexy,
every chance we get,
and definitely do it in public!

Public displays of affection
for The Truth will be the most
played videos on YouTube.

I want to know The Truth.
I believe that we can make it.
I want to know the truth
of the matter that makes us whole,
and the matter of truth
that makes us holy.

When we launch truth
from a monstrous slingshot
through a roofless valley
with our heads cocked,
we'll hear it ricochet
from the waves
between the walls

of our canyon,
and truth will be the song
of that ricochet,
a vibration in balance
as we work our bodies
like a tuning fork
to pitch the forgotten harmony
corked in our spirit.

Skinning Midnight

She looks steel
in that blue dress,
her curves, swaying
every man in the room.
Dropping them
to their balls.

From the bar,
through whiskey,
I watch her work,
watch charm
spilling from her,
like ice filling
a bartender's well.
From my seat
I can see
the slipping
distance
between us.

She holds a room
better than she holds
a lover. At home
when her dress is peeled
off like midnight
carefully skinned,
she puts her back
toward me in bed,
her sharp side,
like a tattooed glacier.

Her nape is neon
humming, a closing
sign.

Bad Sink

got a bad sink
on my shoulders

pipes backed up
like eyes be

Virginia Woolf's
pockets
waiting
for the river

like nose be
Sylvia Plath's
sarcophagus
hearth

like chest be
Gertrude Stein's
echolalia

but my bones
are just bones.

Mariana

Your rocks glass is still
here, an empty fist
on the coffee table, just lip
and fingerprints, you didn't leave
a swig.

When you speak our truth,
your eyes become
kettle-black, the bottom
of the Mariana, a sailor's eclipse.

I am cartographer searching
for the spot I marked, the X
I thought I'd never come back to,
but here I am, at your feet,
with my skinny shovel
and a pile of beach,
flocked in a V, in breach
of our emotional contract,
a betrayal of self-permission
to hold off love on contact
'cause it's not the right timing,
it's never the right timing.

Our misfire runs me rough
like vessel diesel,
crude with karmic irony
filling the oil-pan
on the sofa between us.

You are slick and deflecting.
My tongue-flick breaks things.
Tattoos inside our lips
are armor when we kiss.

When you left, the bottle
wasn't empty. You're gone
now, decomposing darkness.

In your memory,
know me more than stick-figure
on the doorstep, or drab hallway
on the back of your plaid jacket.

Know our unfolding
intimate.

Know my fingers
curled around yours,
a glass fist, that will never
land a punch.

Reclamantra

for Jon Sands

The only cure for writer's block
is not giving a fuck
about writing shit poems.

"Not-Giving-A-Fuckness"
must be harnessed
and ridden into the work!

Picture me up there
on its back, waving pages
of false starts and lame stanzas
howling,
"I don't give a fuuuuuck"
as my mantra.

This is reclamation
stepping out of the dark
with a head on a stick,
face crumpled
like the shittiest poem
ever written.

I step to mangled metaphors
been ugly up my journal like,
      "Guess what, motherfuckers"
you will be the crap,
you will be the shit
that my crap pooped out
'cause I'm tired of sitting around

scared to write
something that scares me,
tired of the suck,
of the cliché wishy-wash, passé,
they're all gonna laugh,
they're all gonna laugh, and
    no one will ever laugh,
        at that.

I need a backhoe and bulldozer
to buck down these barriers.
Mazes and black holes
keep shifting me into
shit mode.

The *fear* of writing a bad poem
is the punishment. It's the debilitating
whip I swing for my penance
that has me gripping the pen
too tight, not the words.

So I say to you—
inspiration eater,
killer in me,
with your can't do it
and give up

    "I will write shit and love it,
    hold it to my chest

and stain my favorite shirt,
smear it all over the page!"

But when the shit turns,
let the fertile in it lead me astray,
let it walk me
'til the squawking
in my knees calls harmony
with larks on the lake,
walk me a mile out of my shoes
just to leave it all behind,
behind the mirror is slate,
I'm out on a dreamscape,
scrape my wings clean of rust,
beat the moths from my closet,
stick-bones swingin' skin
back to body now I'm finding
something to feel -

a heartbeat syncing,
sinkholes plot the course
to the existence I've escaped,
I take to connect that one dot
lingering off page

.

a distant moon-gripped cave
swallowing light like pride,
lunar lozenge on my tongue
to rebalance my tides

.

sway these ocean limbs
back to solid frame,
let the rhythm in the ride
be what I write

.

reclaimed.

Notes

"Launching The Whale" appeared first in *Drawn To The Light,* and "Trespass" appeared first in *Bestiary Magazine.*

About the Author

Matt Gano is a native of Washington State. He grew up eating dust east of the Cascades. He has been writing and teaching professionally since 2004. In 2011, he was invited to lecture as a guest speaker for The Juilliard School in NYC and performed as a featured poet for "Page Meets Stage," at the Bowery Poetry Club. In 2009, he was Writer-in-Residence at the Lee Shau Kee School of Creativity in Hong Kong and led creative writing workshops the previous year for the Youth Creativity Summit in Seoul, Korea. He has represented Seattle at the National Poetry Slam multiple years and is the 2008 Seattle Grand-Slam champion. Matt has worked as a national slam team coach and workshop instructor for Youth Speaks and is currently a senior Artist-in-Residence with Seattle Arts and Lectures, Writers in the Schools. His previously published work includes chapbooks: *Up From the Mine, Bones For The Builder, Music Maker, Welcome Home, I Eight the Infinite* and *Art Barker*. A poetry LP entitled *Music Maker*, and a live recording entitled *A Giant's Pulse*.

Made in the USA
Middletown, DE
29 October 2020